SCIENCE
FUN
ELECTRICITY

A DORLING KINDERSLEY BOOK

Project Editor Linda Martin
Editor Jenny Vaughan
Art Editor Peter Bailey
Designer Mark Regardsoe
Photography Dave King

First published in Great Britain in 1991 by
Dorling Kindersley Limited,
9 Henrietta Street, London WC2E 8PS

Paperback edition
2 4 6 8 10 9 7 5 3 1

A CIP catalogue record for this book is available
from the British Library

ISBN 0-7513-58207

Reproduced in Hong Kong by Bright Arts
Printed in Belgium by Proost

SCIENCE
FUN
ELECTRICITY

Written by
Neil Ardley

DORLING KINDERSLEY
LONDON • NEW YORK • MOSCOW • SYDNEY

What is electricity?

Electric travel
Some electric trains travel at very high speeds. This Japanese train can travel at over 200 kilometres an hour.

Electricity causes the lightning we see in the sky and it powers the fastest trains in the world. Without it, our lives would be very different. One kind of electricity, called "current electricity", powers electric motors, which drive machines. Current electricity also makes light bulbs, televisions, telephones and many other everyday things work. The other kind of electricity is called "static electricity". You can make this kind yourself.

Sticky balloons
You can "charge" balloons with static electricity by rubbing them on a woollen sweater. The balloons will then stick on ceilings, on walls, and even on you!

Power in the home

All around our homes we have "power points" where we can pick up the electricity we need to run machines, like this hair drier.

Water power

Current electricity is made in power stations. This one works using water from a dam. Electricity made this way is called "hydroelectric power".

⚠ This sign means **take care**. You should ask an adult to help you with this step of the experiment.

Be a safe scientist

Follow all the directions carefully and always take care, especially with glass, scissors and matches. Never put anything in your mouth or eyes. Remember that the electricity from power points and light sockets can kill you. **Never** play with electric plugs and switches, power points or electric machines.

Take care when you use 9-volt batteries in experiments as the wires can get very hot after a while.

If you use matchsticks to help connect batteries, they should **always** be used ones.

Batteries and bulbs

Most batteries and bulbs shown in this book are 3 volts. But, for most experiments, it does not matter what size they are. Bulbs should normally be about the same "voltage" as the battery. If you need anything different, the instructions say so.

Bending water

Use a balloon to make electricity, and then see the weird effect it has on water. The kind of electricity that you make is called "static" electricity. It is not the same as the electricity in your home. Static electricity "attracts" things, or draws them towards it.

You will need:

Balloon   Balloon pump

1 Pump up the balloon and tie a knot in the neck.

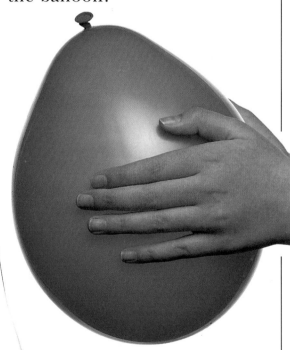

3 Hold the balloon near a smooth stream of water from a tap. The water bends towards the balloon!

2 Rub the balloon on a woollen jumper.

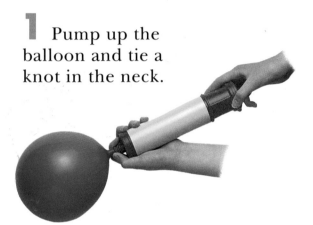

Rubbing an object can give it static electricity. Woollen clothes work best, in dry weather.

Static electricity in the balloon attracts the water. If the balloon gets wet, it loses electricity and the bending stops.

Crazy balloons

Static electricity does not always attract objects. It can "repel" them, or push them apart. Use two balloons to show how this can happen.

You will need:

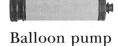
Two balloons

Balloon pump

Thread

Sheet of stiff paper

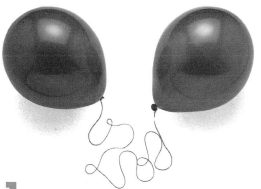

1 Pump up the balloons. Tie knots in their necks and fix the thread to them.

2 Rub the balloons on a woollen jumper. Lift them up. They float apart!

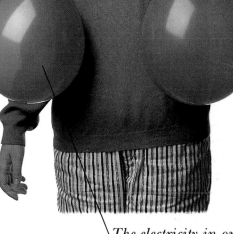

The electricity in one balloon repels the electricity in the other.

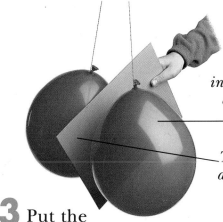

Electricity in the balloons attracts them to the paper.

Take the paper away - and the balloons fly apart again.

3 Put the paper between the balloons. They both stick to it.

This way and that

When something has static electricity in it, we say it has a "charge". There are two kinds of charge – "positive" and "negative". These different charges attract or repel each other.

You will need:

Plastic pen

Thread

Clean, dry handkerchief

Glass bottle

Plastic bottle

Tie the bottle firmly so the thread does not slip.

1 Tie a piece of thread around a plastic bottle and hang it up.

The plastic bottle gets a negative charge of static electricity.

2 Rub the top of the bottle with the handkerchief.

The pen also gets a negative charge, because it is also made of plastic.

3 Rub the plastic pen with the handkerchief.

Make sure you rub the pen really hard.

4 Hold the pen near the bottle. The bottle swings away from it.

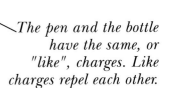

The pen and the bottle have the same, or "like", charges. Like charges repel each other.

If the glass bottle has a plastic top, make sure you remove it.

5 Now hang up the glass bottle and rub it with a handkerchief.

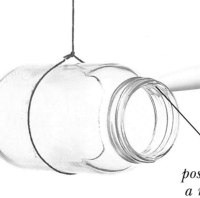

6 Rub the pen again. Hold it near the bottle. The bottle swings towards it.

The glass bottle has a positive charge. The pen has a negative charge. "Unlike" charges attract each other.

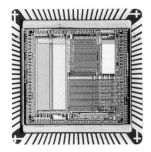

Charged chips

Microchips, or "chips", are used in computers, calculators and many other electric machines. A chip is only the size of a fingernail, but, inside it, there are millions of tiny parts. These store electric charges that make the chip work.

Jumping jacks

There is an invisible "electric field" around anything with an electric charge. It makes static electricity appear in objects near it. See how this works by making some paper people do crazy jumps.

You will need:

Balloon pump

Stiff paper

Pen

Scissors

Balloon

1 Draw some small people on the paper.

2 Cut them out.

3 Place them on a table top.

4 Pump up the balloon and tie a knot in the neck.

5 Rub the balloon on a woollen jumper. This will give the balloon a negative electric charge.

6 Hold the balloon about 10 cm above the people. They will jump up and down several times!

Anything in the balloon's electric field gets a positive charge and is attracted to the balloon.

The balloon attracts the people. When they actually touch it, they get a negative charge and are repelled.

The people jump up and down as they are attracted and repelled, again and again.

Electric pictures
In television cameras and in televisions, tiny electric charges are moved around by electric fields. These charges make pictures show on our screens.

Magic wand

Be a magician and use the power of static electricity to make silver balls dance. With a pencil as a magic wand, scatter the balls - without touching them.

You will need:

Glass or plastic bowl

Silver balls used for cake decoration

LP disc

Sharp pencil

Clean, dry handkerchief

Use an old disc that you do not want to keep!

1 Rub the disc with the handkerchief to give it an electric charge.

2 Put the disc on the glass or plastic bowl.

Some parts of the disc get a higher electric charge than others. These parts attract the balls.

3 Gently drop a few silver balls on the disc. They roll about and then suddenly stop.

4 Bring the pencil towards the disc. As soon as the point gets near a ball, it leaps away and dances round the disc!

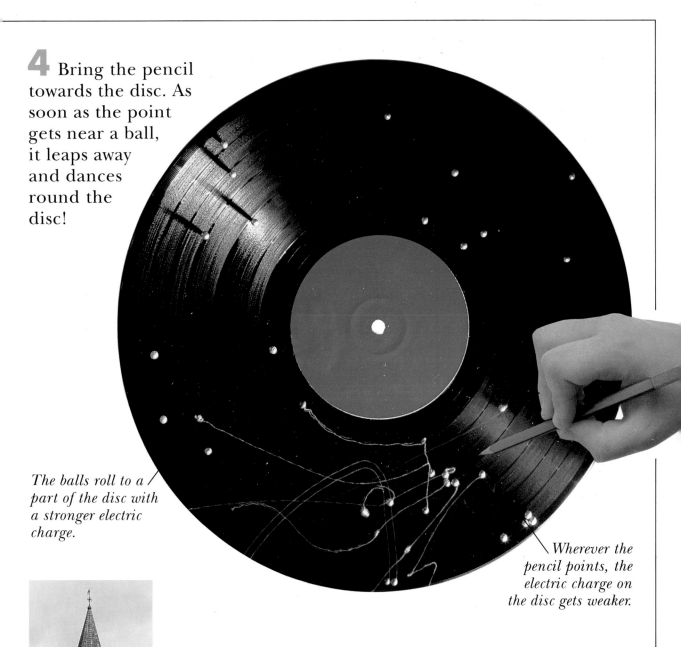

The balls roll to a part of the disc with a stronger electric charge.

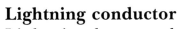

Wherever the pencil points, the electric charge on the disc gets weaker.

Lightning conductor

Lightning happens because thunder clouds have a strong electric charge in them. The pointed rod of a lightning conductor weakens the charge in the clouds, so lightning may not strike at all. If lightning does strike, it hits the conductor and travels safely to the ground.

Charge detector

Can you test for static electricity? Build a simple detector and use it to test a plastic comb. Your detector shows that static electricity can travel. It can go right through your body.

You will need:

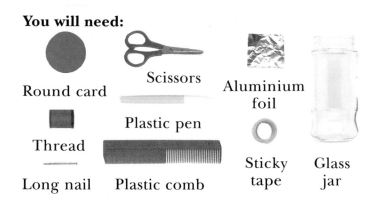

Round card

Scissors

Aluminium foil

Thread

Plastic pen

Long nail

Plastic comb

Sticky tape

Glass jar

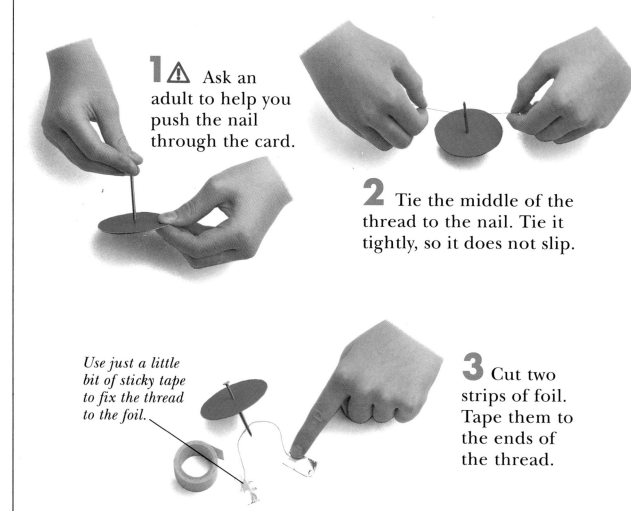

1 ⚠ Ask an adult to help you push the nail through the card.

2 Tie the middle of the thread to the nail. Tie it tightly, so it does not slip.

Use just a little bit of sticky tape to fix the thread to the foil.

3 Cut two strips of foil. Tape them to the ends of the thread.

4 Tape the card to the jar, with the foil strips hanging down inside. This is your detector.

The comb gets a negative charge of electricity.

5 Make sure your hair is dry. Comb it hard, several times.

Electricity travels from the comb down the nail and into the strips.

6 Run the comb along the head of the nail. The foil strips move apart. This shows there is static electricity in the comb.

The electricity gives both strips a negative charge, so they repel each other.

Continued on next page

7 Now grip the top of the nail. The two foil strips collapse and hang straight down.

The static electricity runs out of the strips, up the nail, through your body and down to the ground.

Electricity cannot flow through plastic, so the strips keep their charge.

8 Comb your hair and run the comb along the nail. When the strips move, touch the nail with a plastic pen. Now, they do not collapse.

Sparkling jumpers
Have you ever heard a crackling noise when you pull your jumper over your head? In the dark, you may even see sparks. This is caused by charges leaping through the air between the jumper and your head. Your hair may stand on end too. This is because each hair gets the same charge, and they all repel each other.

Continued from previous page

Simple circuit

So far, all your experiments have been with one kind of electricity, the sort we call "static". Now find out about "current" electricity. This is the kind we use every day.

You will need:

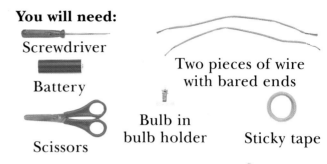

Screwdriver

Battery

Scissors

Two pieces of wire with bared ends

Bulb in bulb holder

Sticky tape

1 Fix one end of each wire to the bulb holder.

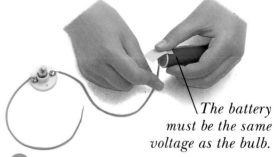

The battery must be the same voltage as the bulb.

2 Tape one of the wires to the base of the battery.

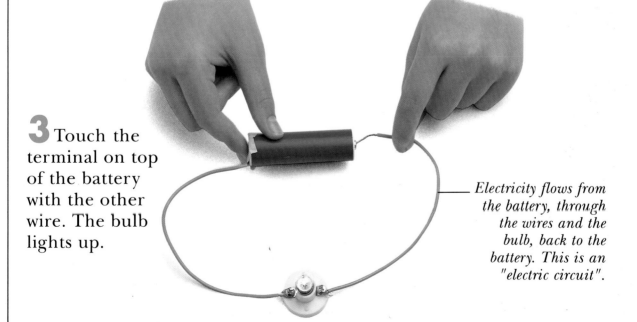

3 Touch the terminal on top of the battery with the other wire. The bulb lights up.

Electricity flows from the battery, through the wires and the bulb, back to the battery. This is an "electric circuit".

Stop or go

Which kinds of materials can electricity flow through? Build a tester to find out. Anything electricity flows through is called a "conductor". Anything it will not flow through is an "insulator".

You will need:

 Battery

 Bulb holder with bulb

Sticky tape

 Scissors

Screwdriver

 Two drawing pins

Piece of cork

 Collection of metal and non-metal objects.

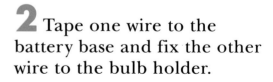 Three pieces of wire with bared ends

1 Twist the ends of two wires around the drawing pins. Push the drawing pins into the cork.

Use the screwdriver to fix the wires to the bulb holder.

2 Tape one wire to the battery base and fix the other wire to the bulb holder.

Make sure that the wires are firmly fixed to the battery and bulb holder.

3 Fix the third wire to the terminal on top of the battery, and to the bulb holder.

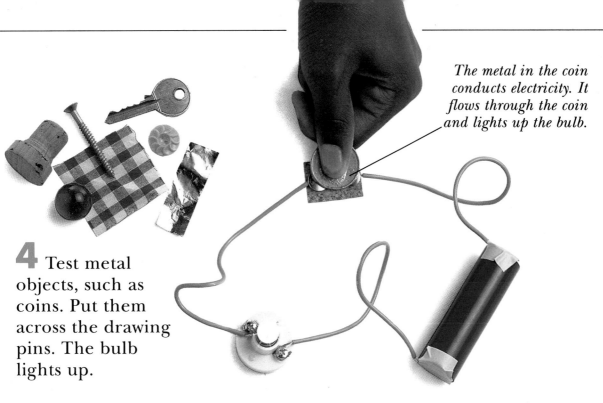

The metal in the coin conducts electricity. It flows through the coin and lights up the bulb.

4 Test metal objects, such as coins. Put them across the drawing pins. The bulb lights up.

5 Test objects that are not made of metal. Electricity cannot flow through these and the bulb will not light up.

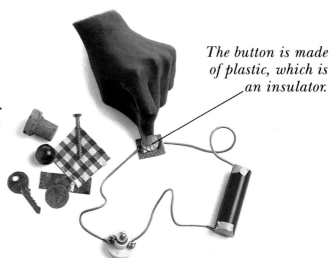

The button is made of plastic, which is an insulator.

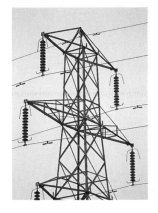

Power and Pylons
Electricity comes to our homes through metal cables supported by tall pylons. The cables hang under long insulators. These stop the powerful electric current passing from the cables into the pylons. Never try to climb a pylon as you could kill yourself.

Simple switch

Make an electric switch and use it to turn an electric current on and off. This switch works in the same way as the switches you have in your home for turning lights on and off.

You will need:

Paperclip

A home-made tester, (see pages 20 and 21)

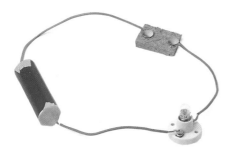

1 Check the tester to make sure it is working properly.

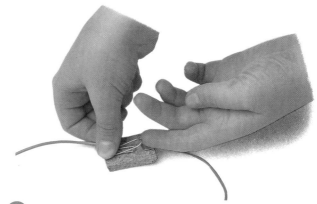

2 Fix the paperclip around one drawing pin. Ask an adult to bend it, so it does not touch the other one.

When the clip touches both drawing pins, it makes a complete electric circuit.

3 The paperclip is your switch. Press it, and the bulb lights up. Let it go, and the bulb goes out.

When the clip springs back, the circuit is broken. The bulb cannot light.

Crackles and sparks

A strong electric current can travel through air. See how it makes sparks! It also makes invisible rays. You can detect these, using a radio.

You will need:

Two used matches

 9-volt battery

Sticky tape

Steel file

 Two pieces of wire with bared ends

Radio

1 Connect the wires to the battery. Use the matches to help fix them firmly.

2 Tape the end of one wire to the handle of the file.

3 Put the radio near the file and turn it on. Stroke the end of the other wire along the file.

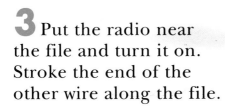

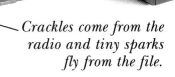

Crackles come from the radio and tiny sparks fly from the file.

Electric storm
A flash of lightning is a huge electric spark. It happens when electricity leaps between thunder clouds, or even between thunder clouds and the ground. When lightning strikes, it can cause crackles on the radio.

Numbers game

How good are your friends at mental arithmetic? Build a machine to test them. The machine has a bulb which lights up when they get the answer to a sum right. Start by making up four sums and working out the answers.

You will need:

Screwdriver

Sticky tape

Card

Eight paper fasteners

Bulb and bulb holder

Scissors

Battery

Pen

Seven pieces of wire with bared ends

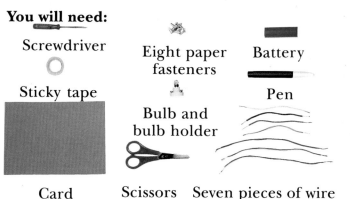

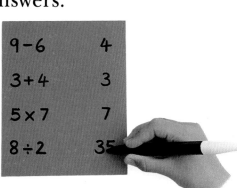

1 Write your sums on the front of the card. But put each answer beside the wrong sum.

9 – 6   4
3 + 4   3
5 × 7   7
8 ÷ 2   35

2 ⚠ Ask an adult to help you push paper fasteners through the front of the card.

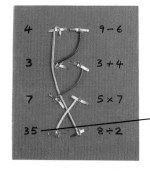

On the back, write the same sums and answers, but put the answers first.

3 Turn the card over. Use four of the wires to connect up each sum with the right answer.

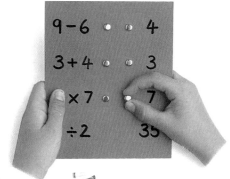

4 Connect the fifth wire between the battery and the bulb holder.

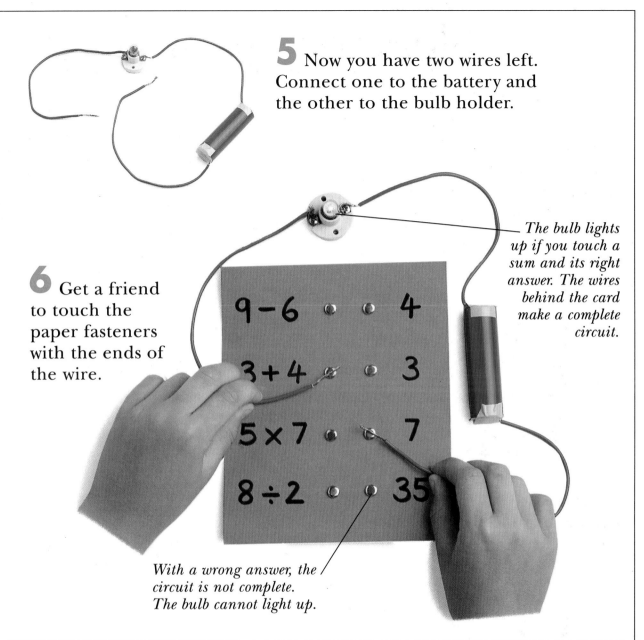

5 Now you have two wires left. Connect one to the battery and the other to the bulb holder.

The bulb lights up if you touch a sum and its right answer. The wires behind the card make a complete circuit.

6 Get a friend to touch the paper fasteners with the ends of the wire.

9 – 6   4

3 + 4   3

5 × 7   7

8 ÷ 2   35

With a wrong answer, the circuit is not complete. The bulb cannot light up.

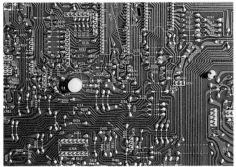

Printed circuits
This is a "circuit board". These are in computers, calculators and many other electric machines. Patterns of lines are printed on the board. The lines act like wires and carry electricity. It flows along lines to link different parts in the machine.

Wobblers beware!

Do you have a steady hand? Find out by building a detector that lights up if you wobble. Use it to test yourself and your friends.

You will need:

Two lids Length of bare, stiff wire Scissors

Bulb holder and bulb Plasticine Three pieces of wire with bared ends

Sticky tape Battery Screwdriver

Make plenty of bends in the bare, stiff wire.

1 Fill the lids with plasticine. Push one end of the stiff wire into each lid.

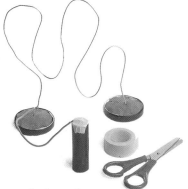

2 Fix one of the three coated wires to the stiff wire and to the battery.

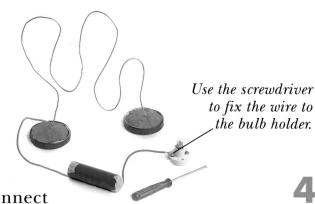

Use the screwdriver to fix the wire to the bulb holder.

3 Connect one of the other wires to the battery and to the bulb holder.

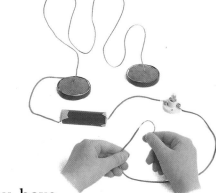

4 You have one wire left. Fix one end of it to the bulb holder. Make the other end into a loop.

5 Hook the loop around the stiff wire. Try to move the loop along the bends without letting the wires touch each other.

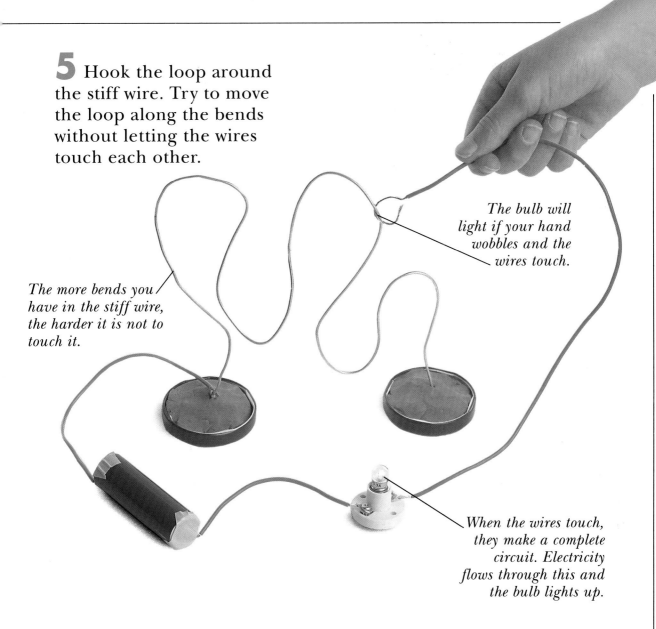

The bulb will light if your hand wobbles and the wires touch.

The more bends you have in the stiff wire, the harder it is not to touch it.

When the wires touch, they make a complete circuit. Electricity flows through this and the bulb lights up.

Electric ride
This fairground car has a metal strip which picks up an electric current from overhead wires. When the strip touches the wires, electricity flows to the car's motor, which turns the wheels. Never touch any overhead wires, as you could get a harmful electric shock.

Salt splitter

Electricity can do amazing things to salt and water. These everyday materials are partly made up of gases. An electric current can split the salt and water apart and let the gases out.

You will need

9-volt battery

Bulb holder and bulb (about 3 volts)

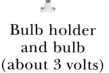
Three pieces of wire with bared ends

Glass of water

Aluminium foil

Sticky tape

Teaspoon of salt

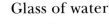
Two used matches

Screwdriver

Scissors

1 Cut out two squares of foil. Tape them to the ends of two wires.

2 Using the matches, fix one of these wires to the battery and the other to the bulb holder.

3 Connect up the third piece of wire between the bulb holder and the battery.

The bulb does not light up. Electricity does not flow very well through pure water.

4 Put the foil squares in the water. Do not let them touch each other.

5 Add a little salt to the water and stir it. The bulb lights up as the salt dissolves.

The electric current splits up the salt and the water, creating bubbles.

Electricity passes easily through salty water. The bulb lights up.

6 Bubbles of gas form on the foil squares. This is where the electric current goes into and leaves the salty water.

Picture credits
(Abbreviation key: B=below, C=centre, L=left, R-right, T=top)

Chris Fairclough Colour Library: 15BL; Pete Gardner: 6BL, 7CR; Malvin van Gelderen: 21BL; The Image Bank: 6TL, 7TL, 13BL, 23BL; Dave King: 18BL; Science Photo Library/ George Bernard: 11BL; Simon Fraser: 25BL; Zefa: 27BL

Picture research Paula Cassidy and Rupert Thomas

Production Louise Barratt

Dorling Kindersley would like to thank Claire Gillard for editorial assistance; Mrs Bradbury, the staff and children of Allfarthing Junior School, Wandsworth, especially Melanie Best, Benny Grebot, Stacey Higgs, Sam Miller, Robin Raggett, Anna Rimoldi and David Tross; Mela Macgregor, Katie Martin, Nicola Ryan, Susanna Scott and Natasha Shepherd.